Strong and Courageous

Encouragement for Families
Touched by Autism

Stephanie Murphy

WESTBOW
P R E S S®
A DIVISION OF THOMAS NELSON
& ZONDERVAN

WestBow Press books may be ordered through booksellers or by contacting:

WestBow Press
A Division of Thomas Nelson & Zondervan
1663 Liberty Drive
Bloomington, IN 47403
www.westbowpress.com
1 (866) 928-1240

ISBN: 978-1-5127-7001-8 (sc)
ISBN: 978-1-5127-7002-5 (hc)
ISBN: 978-1-5127-7000-1 (e)

Library of Congress Control Number: 2016921544

Print information available on the last page.

WestBow Press rev. date: 1/20/2017

To _____

From _____

Dedication

I dedicate this book to my daughter, son-in-law, and grandson. They are the strongest and most courageous family I know!

Lord, Your word tells us to be strong and courageous. Thank You for the strength and courage You give to those who invite You to walk beside them on their journey.

Contents

Introduction

Let me tell you about my beautiful, wonderful grandson. He came into our world on a mild January day in 2008. There he was, my Floridian grandson, joining ranks with my two older grandchildren, who lived in Illinois.

I spent my first week with the little guy, helping his mother during her recuperation and both parents as they adjusted to parenting their first child. By his second week, his mommy told me he could come for a sleepover. That weekend began a tradition of him spending one night each weekend at his grandparents' home. My bond with my grandson began very early and continues to grow with each passing week.

My grandson is a very entertaining little boy. He loves to play chase, watch his favorite movies, sing, and swim in the family pool. Trains and cars or anything with moving parts fascinate him.

This is my beautiful, wonderful grandson! When I look lovingly into his eyes, I see him—not the autism. He is so much more than the autism. He is a joy, a gift, and a wonder. My wish is that he reaches his full God-given potential, is happy, and feels loved and accepted.

When my grandson turned three, I received the news that he had been diagnosed with autism spectrum disorder (ASD). My initial response was one of deep sadness and despair. Family members go through stages of grief when a child is diagnosed with autism. Some become stuck there. Others move from grief to action and later, to acceptance and hope. It is a journey, and each person navigates the road differently.

My reaction was to voraciously read every book I could find about ASD. Although I was a marriage and family therapist and had counseled many families dealing with autism in my private practice, this was different! This was *my* grandchild, and I felt the weight of worry as I tried to make sense of it all in my own life.

Fortunately, we were able to find a physician who was a specialist in the treatment of autism and utilized biomedical and nutritional methods. We also discovered a program that focused on one-on-one interaction and the idea of having us join the child in his world so he could join us in ours.

Although my grandson has experienced phenomenal success, there have also been setbacks. Most of the time he interacts with others well, uses good and frequent eye contact, and happily sings his way through his day. At other times, especially during transitions, it is a bit more difficult for him. I have learned that he will have good days and bad days, which is not that much different from all of us. These are the times when parents and grandparents need to fully accept their child while embracing the hope that he is progressing toward his full potential.

I experienced a sense of relief when my grandson adapted to his school program and learned to read quite well. It's hard for grandparents to let our little ones grow up. Although they need our careful supervision, it's important that we not cheat them out of the sense of competence that comes from learning to do something independently. Each new step gives them hope and confidence that they can reach the next one.

I am now at peace with my grandson's autism. I am full of hope and do not have the desperation of needing him to be healed or cured. He is God's precious creation, and I have concluded that God loves him even more than I do. With that realization, I can rest in the confidence that God has everything under control! I am grateful God trusted me to be this precious child's grandmother—to love and care for him in the way he needs.

My hope and prayer for families touched by autism is that they will not spend their days grieving for what could have been but will rejoice in what is, will celebrate the beautiful gift they have been given, and realize just how strong and courageous they truly are!

Chapter 1

Strong and Courageous

"Have I not commanded you? Be strong and courageous. Do not be afraid; do not be discouraged, for the Lord your God will be with you wherever you go."

—Joshua 1:9 (NIV)

I just caught a glimpse of the holiday card that still hangs on my refrigerator long past the season. I leave it there because I like to look at the pictures on it— pictures of my grandson, daughter, and son-in-law. Tonight, as it caught my eye, the words *courageous* and *strong* went through my mind. Yes, they are the most courageous and strong family I know!

I've met some others these past few years but I'm not as familiar with their stories. As I look at my grandson's sweet smile, I can't help but think of how brave he is as he maneuvers through life on the "spectrum." That's what the professionals call it, but to families who have children with autism, each case is a bit different. Others call it a "puzzle" because there are no clearcut answers or solutions. Each family walks its own unique path while at the same time seeking some common ground with others.

They are courageous because they face uncertainties, ups and downs, and successes and failures. You might say, "Well we all do," and you're right, but this is different. No one really understands unless their lives have been touched by autism. My grandson's family doesn't give up! They don't quit on him! If one treatment doesn't give the results they were hoping for, they try another— and another! That's what you do when there's no set treatment that helps everyone.

They are brave because they dare to give their child the most normal childhood possible. They play together, laugh together, and sing. They go to Disney and to the mountains. They play basketball, swim, and ride bikes. And they go to the beach and to church. They don't allow their challenges to keep them from having fun and enjoying each other.

Yes, they have expenses— special supplements, diets, and therapies that insurance doesn't always cover. There are private schools and camps. What do they do? They could complain and cry about it but they just work harder. As they take on extra work, they are acutely aware that they need to protect their availability as parents, so they choose work that offers them flexibility. Sometimes they ask family for help, and that's okay. I'm sure they'd rather not but do it for their child's best interests. They are his advocate.

So maybe you're getting an idea of why I say they are strong and courageous. They need our support and they need our prayers. God has promised them, as He has promised all of us, that He is with us wherever we go. Wherever our path goes, He is there waiting for us to trust in Him and to draw upon His strength.

Many times throughout the Bible, God has commanded His people to have courage. Courage means having confidence and faith in Him. When we trust Him, we are able to live a life that is full of courage! When our hope is in Him, our strength is renewed!

Be strong and courageous. Do not be afraid or terrified because of them, for the Lord your God goes with you; he will never leave you nor forsake you.

Deuteronomy 31:6 (NIV)

So do not fear, for I am with you; do not be dismayed, for I am your God. I will strengthen you and help you; I will uphold you with my righteous right hand.

Isaiah 41:10 (NIV)

He gives strength to the weary and increases the power of the weak. Even youths grow tired and weary, and young men stumble and fall; but those who hope in the Lord will renew their strength. They will soar on wings like eagles; they will run and not grow weary, they will walk and not be faint.

Isaiah 40:29–31 (NIV)

Reflections

1. What are some ways you and your family show strength and courage in your day-to-day life?

_____

_____

_____

_____

2. Whom do you go to when you feel afraid or discouraged?

_____

_____

_____

_____

3. How does your faith in God strengthen you as you walk this path with your child?

_____

_____

_____

_____

Chapter 2

The Diagnosis

The Lord is close to the brokenhearted and saves those who
are crushed in spirit.

—Psalm 34:18 (NIV)

Crushed! It hit me like a ton of bricks from out of nowhere and
fell on me as I was simply walking along in life. At first I couldn't
believe it. I thought the diagnosis must be incorrect. Later I
questioned how this could be happening to our family.

During those early weeks and months, I spent numerous hours
weeping before God and bargaining with Him. If only He would
heal my grandson, I would work harder, pray more, and draw
closer to Him—as if I were in some way responsible, as if it were
about me. How self-centered we become sometimes, thinking
everything is about us! Although God has lessons for each of us
to learn in these types of situations, He may never reveal, on this
earth, the depth and breadth of His sovereign purposes.

Some people struggle with faulty thoughts and perceptions
as they try to put the pieces together and make sense of their
situation. They feel God has abandoned them, hates them or is
punishing them for some long ago sin. It may become difficult

for them to pray as they perceive a distance in their once close relationship with God.

Early on, I tried to figure all of this out—tried to fix it. I stayed awake until the early hours of the morning reading every book I could find about autism. To my dismay, there were no clearcut answers to be found. Even though distinct diagnostic criteria describe autism, every case is different, and every child is unique.

Families who have been touched by autism are on their own unique journey. Part of this journey is learning to put our trust in God's sovereignty, knowing He is close to us when we are brokenhearted—when our spirits are crushed. May God bless you as you look to Him for help as your family walks through the uncertainties of autism!

Your heart can be crushed when you hear the words, "Your child has autism." God wants to strengthen you and comfort your hurting heart. He wants to give you hope!

They will have no fear of bad news; their hearts are steadfast, trusting in the Lord.

Psalm 112:7 (NIV)

I have set the Lord continually before me; Because He is at my right hand, I will not be shaken.

Psalm 16:8 (NASB)

Be anxious for nothing, but in everything by prayer and supplication with thanksgiving let your requests be made known to God. And the peace of God, which surpasses all comprehension, will guard your hearts and your minds in Christ Jesus.

Philippians 4:6–7 (NASB)

Reflections

1. How did you feel when you first heard the words, "Your child has autism"?

_____

_____

_____

_____

2. During this time, did you find yourself blaming others, yourself, or God in an effort to make sense of things? Explain.

_____

_____

_____

_____

3. How difficult has it been to trust God's sovereignty in your life?

_____

_____

_____

_____

Chapter 3

Moving through Grief

He got up, rebuked the wind and said to the waves, "Quiet! Be still!" Then the wind died down and it was completely calm.

—Mark 4:39 (NIV)

I started writing about God's healing love after my grandson was diagnosed with autism. It wasn't my first response but was the place God brought me to. I needed God's healing love to calm my storm of grief. He was faithful and brought me from a position of despair and grief to a place of peace and acceptance.

Mark 4:35–41 tells the story of Jesus calming a stormy sea when His disciples came to Him for help. They didn't come in perfect faith. In fact, they came in fear. Jesus met them where they were and understood their need for peace and calm. The journey through grief is a storm. Early on, most of us realize we can't find peace in our own strength. We need God's help!

It is important for families who are touched by autism not to become paralyzed by grief and get stuck there. There is so much ahead of you on your journey. You can't afford to use up your energy and resources by allowing your focus to remain on grief. I'm not saying you should not work through your feelings of sadness and loss. Take time to feel your feelings and to reach out to trusted friends and family who will validate those feelings. Then allow God to heal your heart!

As Jesus met His disciples where they were—afraid and dismayed—He will meet you right where you are. I found I didn't have to put my anchor down in the stormy waters of grief. In other words, I didn't have to get stuck there. With God's help, I was able to keep on going and reach the shore of acceptance and hope.

My prayer is that God will shower you with His healing love as you move from grief to acceptance. May He quiet your storm and give you His peace!

It is easy to become stuck in grief as you try to work through your feelings of sadness, but your Heavenly Father wants to quiet your storm and comfort your heart with His unfailing love. He wants to give you peace.

Though the mountains be shaken and the hills removed, yet my unfailing love for you will not be shaken nor my covenant of peace be removed, says the Lord, who has compassion on you.

Isaiah 54:10 (NIV)

He heals the brokenhearted and binds up their wounds.

Psalm 147:3 (NIV)

Praise be to the God and Father of our Lord Jesus Christ, the Father of compassion and the God of all comfort, who comforts us in all our troubles, so that we can comfort those in any trouble with the comfort we ourselves receive from God.

2 Corinthians 1:3–4 (NIV)

Reflections

1. How difficult has it been for you not to become *stuck* in your grief?

_____

_____

_____

_____

2. What has helped you move through this stage in a healthy way?

_____

_____

_____

_____

3. In what ways have you allowed your Heavenly Father to comfort you and to give you peace?

_____

_____

_____

_____

Chapter 4

What Happens Now?

In all your ways acknowledge Him, And He will make your
paths straight.

—Proverbs 3:6 (NASB)

So you've accepted the reality of autism in your family. What
happens now? You may feel extremely overwhelmed in the world
of autism. Most of us have heard of it but don't really understand
it in its totality. Then when we start researching, we find it's a bit
different for everyone. It is called "being on the spectrum," but
where on the spectrum?

Part of the ongoing evaluation process is to identify where your
child is on the spectrum, and this can change! With treatment,
some children move quickly to a higher place of functioning
while others progress more slowly. A child may develop well in
one area but require more treatment and time in others.

So, where do you begin? What do you do? I suggest you start
with prayer. Ask God to direct you every step of the way, from
the doctors and therapists you choose to the school your child
will be attending. Many treatments require trial and error. This
can become discouraging if the results are less than what you had
hoped for.

As you begin this journey, ask God to put knowledgeable people in your path who can be a resource to you. Ask for wisdom as you visit schools and research community programs. You will discover that many of the private services are expensive unless they are covered by special programs. Many families have found creative ways to raise funds for these services. While seeking treatment for your child, don't become discouraged when you hit a financial wall. Again, seek God's direction and help.

Don't forget that God cares about you, your family, and your child. He wants you to look to Him for wisdom and help in the midst of life's struggles. During difficult times, I have often prayed and asked God to "go before me and make the crooked places straight." This is my prayer for you and your family as you maneuver the twists and turns of autism!

As the parent of a child with autism, it is normal to feel overwhelmed as you begin your journey. The Bible encourages us to seek God's direction in our lives and assures us He will generously give wisdom to those who ask for it.

If any of you lacks wisdom, you should ask God, who gives generously to all without finding fault, and it will be given to you.

James 1:5 (NIV)

Commit to the Lord whatever you do, and he will establish your plans.

Proverbs 16:3 (NIV)

Trust in the Lord with all your heart and lean not on your own understanding;

Proverbs 3:5 (NIV)

Reflections

1. Describe the situation where you have felt the most overwhelmed.

_____

_____

_____

_____

2. What resources have been helpful in developing your child's treatment plan?

_____

_____

_____

_____

3. How has prayer helped you gain a sense of trust and direction in your life?

_____

_____

_____

_____

Chapter 5

Why?

And we know that God causes all things to work together for good to those who love God, to those who are called according to His purpose.

—Romans 8:28 (NASB)

Even though you have accepted your child's diagnosis, you may still have some nagging questions running through your mind. The "Why?" question is one of them. "Why is this happening to me and my family?" "What good could possibly come from this?"

I certainly could not see all of the good that would come out of our situation, but looking back over the years, it is apparent that much good has come about. You and your family have the opportunity to experience personal, relational, and spiritual growth that would not have been otherwise available. Only those who walk this path truly know what I'm talking about when I make this statement: "Was the growth smooth and easy? No way! Was it life changing? Absolutely!"

Personal growth—patience, unselfishness, unconditional love, and perseverance—involves building character through difficulty. Relational growth is enhanced among parents and other family members as they work together for the welfare of the child. This

17

is won through struggle and adapting to new family dynamics. Many experience a deeper and richer relationship with God as they press into Him and learn to trust in His sovereignty.

It has been a journey filled with many lessons and deep spiritual growth. I have learned to trust God's providence for the future. I have learned to walk more closely with Him and to allow Him to fill me with His peace. So how do I respond to the question "Why?" I may never fully understand why my family has experienced the things it has in this life. I only know that God has meant them for our good.

If your hope has been shaken by the uncertainties of autism or by circumstances beyond your control, I pray you will find renewed hope in God's promise that all things work together for our good. May your hope be renewed for the future He has for you!

We don't always understand God's ways or purposes because, as scripture tells us, they are higher than our ways or thoughts. So we learn to trust Him because we know He is good and loving.

"For I know the plans I have for you," declares the Lord, "plans to prosper you and not to harm you, plans to give you hope and a future."

Jeremiah 29:11 (NIV)

And those who know Your name will put their trust in You, For You, O Lord, have not forsaken those who seek you.

Psalm 9:10 (NASB)

For the foolishness of God is wiser than human wisdom, and the weakness of God is stronger than human strength.

1 Corinthians 1:25 (NIV)

Reflections

1. In what ways have you struggled with the question "Why"?

_____

_____

_____

_____

2. How has your journey brought about positive change and personal growth in your life?

_____

_____

_____

_____

3. In what ways have you learned to trust in God's providence and love and care for you?

_____

_____

_____

_____

Chapter 6

Your *New Normal*

You will keep in perfect peace those whose minds are steadfast, because they trust in you.

—Isaiah 26:3 (NIV)

Change produces anxiety—even positive change! I would like you to keep this in mind as you and your family members adapt to your *new normal*. There will be changes in your lives that you did not plan on or anticipate. You can choose to view your new normal as positive or negative. However, corresponding feelings will follow whatever attitude you decide on. If you choose to think negatively about having to drive your child to various therapies during the week, you will most likely feel sorry for yourself and resent the drain on your time. On the other hand, if you choose to be happy and excited that your child has the opportunity to receive the help of various professionals, you will likely feel more hopeful and grateful.

For many years I counseled people who were experiencing anxiety. They felt powerless and overwhelmed by their circumstances. Their main symptom seemed to be a lack of peace and even fear. A sense of unrest permeated the person's emotional outlook. Many had simply given up!

Your emotions can be tossed about as you experience all of the uncertainties involved in your child's progress. One day, you may be ecstatic when he says a new word. The next day, you may be devastated by a negative test score. Unless you keep your mind steadfastly trusting God, you will feel like you are on an emotional roller coaster. God has promised perfect peace to those who keep their minds stayed on Him.

Your new normal may look crazy to the person who is on the outside looking in. That's okay. Don't worry about the judgment of someone who has never walked in your shoes. Be sure to surround yourself with people who understand what you are going through and are there to give you love and support—not criticism! Your calm spirit will rub off on your child, giving him a feeling of security as he tries to make sense of his world.

May God bless you as you walk this journey with your child. May you find His peace in the midst of your new normal.

During the transitions of our lives, we often feel a sense of unrest and instability. When we know God is unchanging, it gives us a sense of security as we adjust to our new normal.

Jesus Christ is the same yesterday and today and forever.

Hebrews 13:8 (NIV)

Give thanks to the Lord, for he is good; his love endures forever.

Psalm 107:1 (NIV)

The Lord himself goes before you and will be with you; he will never leave you nor forsake you. Do not be afraid; do not be discouraged.

Deuteronomy 31:8 (NIV)

Reflections

1. In what ways have you made peace with your new normal?

   _____

   _____

   _____

   _____

2. List the people in your life who are understanding and supportive of you.

   _____

   _____

   _____

   _____

3. How has God's unfailing love given you a sense of security as you adjust to your new normal?

   _____

   _____

   _____

   _____

Chapter 7

Family Dynamics

God sets the lonely in families,

—Psalm 68:6a (NIV)

Your journey, at times, may feel lonely. It can seem as though your friends don't understand what you're going through. As a family, you must pull together and love and support each other more than ever before!

You are on this path together and your family dynamics will have to change a bit to fit your new situation. This requires communication, patience, and flexibility with each other. Your needs are greater now and, at times, you will have to ask family members for help. Maybe you aren't comfortable with this. After all, you have independently managed your family's life quite well in the past, right?

Extended family members are a resource you can't duplicate with organizations or caregivers. These resources are necessary and serve their purpose when family support is not available or to supplement the family support you have. But if you're fortunate enough to have grandparents, aunts, uncles, siblings, or cousins living nearby, be sure to give them the opportunity to be part of your life.

Notice that I said, "Give them the opportunity to be part of your life." This is very important. Don't manipulate or guilt them into helping but simply make them aware of your specific needs and ask for their assistance. Be sure to express your appreciation and not take them for granted. Remember that they still have their own lives and needs, which are separate from yours. Although they are walking this journey with you and are supporting you along the way, they have their own life path as well.

May God bless you and your family as you work together for the well-being of your child. May you find healthy ways to interact with each other as you work through these changes in your family dynamics.

Our family relationships need to be loving and kind as we work together to encourage each other. As family members relate to one another in gentle and supportive ways, they not only strengthen their bonds but also function as a team. Their child with autism reaps the benefit of having a strong family unit.

Love is patient, love is kind. It does not envy, it does not boast, it is not proud. It does not dishonor others, it is not self-seeking, it is not easily angered, it keeps no record of wrongs.

1 Corinthians 13:4–5 (NIV)

Be completely humble and gentle; be patient, bearing with one another in love.

Ephesians 4:2 (NIV)

Therefore encourage one another and build up one another, just as you also are doing.

1 Thessalonians 5:11 (NASB)

Reflections

1. How have your family members' relationships changed since your child was diagnosed with autism?

_____

_____

_____

_____

2. What are some important ways your extended family provides support and encouragement to you and your child?

_____

_____

_____

_____

3. What are some ways you and your extended family members could improve the quality of your relationships? Boundaries? Communication? Personality differences? Kindness?

_____

_____

_____

_____

Chapter 8

Family Traditions

Behold, how good and how pleasant it is for brothers to dwell
together in unity!

—Psalm 133:1 (NASB)

Over the years, I have treasured my childhood memories of
Christmas and other holidays at my grandparents' home. These
were family traditions, and I could count on them year after year.
The warmth and sense of security I experienced during those
family gatherings are mine to draw upon and to pass down to
my own children.

Traditions foster feelings of closeness and family stability.
They protect our sense of security amidst abrupt changes,
which sometimes come into our lives. Traditions act as
assurances as we deal with the pressures of life. When a family
makes a holiday special, this has a way of making children feel
special too.

Many children with autism like to do things the way they
have always been done. Although we work to help them become
more flexible in daily life, they enjoy the familiarity of specific
activities around holidays. Including extended family in some of

your traditions will give your child great pleasure and enhance his sense of family unity.

May God bless you as you seek to enrich your family unity, stability, and continuity through your own uniquely meaningful and fulfilling family traditions!

The cohesiveness of family gives us a sense of stability as we walk through life. Our traditions and beliefs, passed down from generation to generation, help mold who we are and who we become.

"But if serving the Lord seems undesirable to you, then choose for yourselves this day whom you will serve ... But as for me and my household, we will serve the Lord."

Joshua 24:15 (NIV)

"Honor your father and your mother, as the Lord your God has commanded you, so that you may live long and that it may go well with you in the land the Lord your God is giving you."

Deuteronomy 5:16 (NIV)

Praise the Lord. Blessed are those who fear the Lord, who find great delight in his commands. Their children will be mighty in the land; the generation of the upright will be blessed.

Psalm 112:1–2 (NIV)

Reflections

1. Which treasured holiday traditions from your own childhood have you passed down to your children?

_____

_____

_____

_____

2. Which important beliefs have been passed down from generation to generation in your family?

_____

_____

_____

_____

3. How are you providing a sense of stability and family cohesiveness for your child?

_____

_____

_____

_____

Chapter 9

What Happened to My Social Life?

A friend loves at all times, and a brother is born for a time of adversity.

—Proverbs 17:17 (NIV)

At some point you may ask, "What happened to my social life?" or, "Where are all my friends?" Many people are shocked when they find themselves in this position. After all, they had many friends to socialize with.

You find yourself adapting yet to another *change*. Parenthood, in itself, conjures up changes in our social lives and friendships. Over time, families adapt, create relevant social outlets, and often make new friends who share similar lifestyles.

This same dynamic is present in families who have been touched by autism but with an added dimension. Some of your friends will fade into the background simply because they don't know what to do. Their understanding of autism may be very limited and they are at a loss—not knowing how to relate to you. This is unfortunate and definitely needs to be addressed in our society through more awareness and education about autism.

Churches also need to get on board as a resource for families who have children on the spectrum. We can no longer ignore families who have children with special needs.

One of the churches in my community is an example of what it means to step up to the plate and do something! They provide a monthly respite time for parents called Buddy Break. Each child with special needs is paired with a trained volunteer for a morning of fun activities in the church's gymnasium. My grandson absolutely loves it! He's excited about going and enjoys himself while he is there. This resource also gives parents the opportunity for some much needed time for themselves on a Saturday morning.

Some friends will rally around you even if others choose to go another direction. As time goes by, you will make many new friends who are walking a similar path to yours. You may be surprised how deep and rewarding those friendships can become as you draw upon similar experiences to become united. May God bless your family as you expand your horizons and create fun, supportive, and fulfilling relationships with others.

Stephanie Murphy

Loyal friends are of great worth and walk with us through difficult times. They help us grow and give us love and support. May your life be blessed with many!

A man _that hath_ friends must shew himself friendly: and there is a friend _that_ sticketh closer than a brother.

Proverbs 18:24 (KJV)

"This is My commandment, that you love one another, just as I have loved you. Greater love has no man than this, that one lay down his life for his friends."

John 15:12–13 (NASB)

As iron sharpens iron, so one person sharpens another.

Proverbs 27:17 (NIV)

Reflections

1. How are you feeling about your current social life?

_____

_____

_____

_____

2. Which specific steps could you take to build new friendships?

_____

_____

_____

_____

3. What do you wish your friends could understand about what it means to be a family touched by autism?

_____

_____

_____

_____

Chapter 10

If We Walk a Little Slower

Jesus said, "Let the little children come to me, and do not hinder them, for the kingdom of heaven belongs to such as these."

—Matthew 19:14 (NIV)

While I was recently sitting in the bleachers watching my nine-year-old grandson's baseball game, the words of a poem I wrote kept going through my mind, "If we walk a little slower, they won't lag behind." You see, this was not your average baseball game. The game had only two innings, and the players were not all the same age. Some kids came up to bat in their wheelchairs while others were directed by their own personal buddies. They didn't all look the same or act the same, but one thing was universal, they all had big smiles on their faces!

The coaches generously gave praise and high fives for each child's effort and *success*. Although the successes were not based on typical standards, they were the most beautiful successes I have ever seen! My husband, daughter, and son-in-law joined together to cheer for each child, regardless of which team he or she was on. The crowd rooted enthusiastically for every child, not for a specific team.

We all slowed down that day. We walked a little slower so the children wouldn't lag behind. We adapted the rules to each child's special needs. They had a blast! We had a blast! These precious children left the baseball field feeling alive and part of something important. They left with smiles and a newfound confidence. Their parents experienced the gift of being able to sit in the stands and cheer for their child—something most of us take for granted.

When Jesus admonished His disciples to let the little children come to Him, He slowed down and took the time to give them His love and attention. By doing this, He acknowledged their value. May each of us "slow down" from our busy schedules and validate the importance and worth of the children in our lives. And let's be sure and not forget about those with special needs. They are truly God's gifts to us!

> Behold, children are a gift from the Lord, the fruit of the womb is a reward.
>
> Psalm 127:3 (NASB)

> "Truly I tell you, anyone who will not receive the kingdom of God like a little child will never enter it." And he took the children in his arms, placed his hands on them and blessed them.
>
> Mark 10:15–16 (NIV)

> He took a little child whom he placed among them. Taking the child in his arms, he said to them, "Whoever welcomes one of these little children in my name welcomes me."
>
> Mark 9:36–37 (NIV)

Stephanie Murphy

Reflections

1. List some important ways you can validate your child's worth.

   _____

   _____

   _____

   _____

2. What changes do you need to make in order to _walk a little slower?_

   _____

   _____

   _____

   _____

3. In what ways do you see your child as being a gift from God?

   _____

   _____

   _____

   _____

Chapter 11

Strong in Your Marriage

Two are better than one, because they have a good return
for their labor: If either of them falls down, one can help the
other up.

—Ecclesiastes 4:9–10 (NIV)

Yes, you will experience change in your marriage relationship!
However, the choices you make in the midst of these changes
are what ultimately affect the outcome. You can grow apart and
become conflictual with each other, or you can become stronger.

I have seen couples pull together and support each other
even when their own reservoirs were nearly empty. This comes
from a place of inner strength that only God can provide. In
our own strength, we often fail and give in to self-centeredness
and selfishness. But with God's strength, we can soar above the
difficult circumstances in our lives.

Your commitment to each other and to your marriage will
take you through stressful times as you adjust to parenting your
child. At times, you may have different opinions about your
child's treatment options. One of you may even feel you are
carrying an unfair amount of the responsibility. You need to

be emotionally mature before you can listen to each other and try to understand one another's position rather than becoming defensive or resentful. Communicating with love and respect will protect and strengthen your relationship and preserve your level of intimacy.

The very nature of autism requires that you focus on your child. You can balance this by purposefully staying connected to your spouse. You do this by staying in touch with your spouse's personal interests and with his or her heart. Be sure to plan times where you can be alone together—date nights and one-on-one talks.

Couples who parent a child with autism can have a strong marriage, even in the midst of stress and uncertainty. It requires understanding the unique challenges you face just by the nature of your family dynamics. So don't give up! Your child craves the stability of a loving and secure home as he faces his own challenges. As a couple, you also need the stability of a strong, secure, and supportive relationship with your spouse. This takes a realistic perspective on your circumstances, a commitment to your marriage and family, and a willingness to work at building a solid marriage.

May God bless you as you seek to have a loving, intimate, and strong marriage!

Marriage can be one of life's richest blessings when God is the center of your relationship. I will always remember the wise words spoken by a young Romanian minister during my wedding ceremony, "The more a man has of God, the greater his capacity to love and care for his wife. And the more a woman has of God, the greater her capacity to love and respect her husband."

Nevertheless, each individual among you also is to love his own wife even as himself, and the wife must *see to it* that she respects her husband.

Ephesians 5:33 (NASB)

Husbands, love your wives, just as Christ also loved the church and gave Himself up for her,

Ephesians 5:25 (NASB)

An excellent wife, who can find? For her worth is far above jewels. The heart of her husband trusts in her, And he will have no lack of gain. She does him good and not evil All the days of her life.

Proverbs 31:10–12 (NASB)

Reflections

1. What changes have you experienced in your marriage since your child was diagnosed with autism?

_____

_____

_____

_____

2. What are the things you most appreciate about your husband or wife?

_____

_____

_____

_____

3. How can you work together as a couple to strengthen your marriage?

_____

_____

_____

_____

Chapter 12

Self-Care

Dear friend, I pray that you may enjoy good health and that all may go well with you, even as your soul is getting along well.

—3 John 2 (NIV)

Because the time and emotional drains of raising a child with autism are great, it is important not to neglect your own self-care. You may ask, "How can I indulge in taking time just for myself?" You may be up sporadically throughout the night with your child and then up early in the morning to start your routine. Then it's go, go, go, all day long until you drop into bed at night, physically exhausted and emotionally spent.

It is important for parents of children with autism to learn to *slow down*! So many families go full speed ahead with therapies and forget they have a life outside of autism. It becomes all-consuming! So it's important to realize that it is a *marathon*, not a *sprint*, and whatever you are doing is *enough* for today.

It is imperative to tend to your own emotional, physical, and spiritual health. You have to find time for yourself! Will this be easy? Absolutely not! But with some creativity, you can invest in your own self-care without neglecting your responsibility to care for your child. In fact, it is in your child's best interest for you to be well rested, relaxed, and in a good place spiritually.

If you are married, your spouse is your best ally when it comes to achieving your self-care goals. Be sure and make this a mutual endeavor. Help each other. You can provide precious time for your mate to exercise, spend time with a friend, or have a quiet time for Bible reading and prayer. The time you give each other for these activities is priceless!

If you are lucky enough to have grandparents living nearby, you will most likely be blessed with extra support, possibly allowing you to have a date night with your spouse. I have tried to give my daughter and son-in-law a weekly overnight time when they can go out together and sleep late the next morning. Although there have been times when this was not possible, over the years, I have tried to make it a priority when I am home. It also gives me great quality time with my grandson. It is a double blessing for them and for me.

Here is one word of caution. Be sure to differentiate between healthy self-care and selfishness. You will never find happiness in selfishness. It is a bottomless pit that leaves you empty. You will actually feel fulfilled by doing something for someone else from time to time. You may wonder how this could be possible with all of your family responsibilities, but just try it. Why not do something thoughtful for one of your child's teachers or grandparents? Giving back always enhances our feelings of happiness and purpose.

May God bless you as you endeavor to balance your responsibilities with healthy self-care. As John said in 3 John 2, "I pray that you may enjoy good health and that all may go well with you."

Give yourself permission to rest, laugh, and have fun! It's okay! Love yourself enough to take good care of your body, soul, and spirit.

Then, because so many people were coming and going that they did not even have a chance to eat, he said to them, "Come with me by yourselves to a quiet place and get some rest."

Mark 6:31 (NIV)

I know that there is nothing better for people than to be happy and to do good while they live. That each of them may eat and drink, and find satisfaction in all their toil—this is the gift of God.

Ecclesiastes 3:12–13 (NIV)

After all, no one ever hated their own body, but they feed and care for their body, just as Christ does the church—for we are members of his body.

Ephesians 5:29–30 (NIV)

Reflections

1. What are some creative ways you can enhance the quality of your own self-care?

   _____

   _____

   _____

   _____

2. What are you willing to do to support your spouse's self-care goals?

   _____

   _____

   _____

   _____

3. What are some things you can do for others that will increase your feelings of happiness and purpose?

   _____

   _____

   _____

   _____

Chapter 13

Nurturing Your Spiritual Growth

Draw near to God and He will draw near to you.

—James 4:8a (NASB)

I want to encourage you to nurture your own spiritual growth. You may have a tendency to put this on the back burner as you care for your child with autism. However, I hope you will not minimize the importance of feeding your soul!

As you find time to read God's Word, your spirit will be refreshed, and your personal relationship with Christ will deepen. Making time for prayer is important for all of us, as we seek to live victoriously in this world. Attending church gives us the opportunity to worship God with fellow believers.

You might agree that all of these things sound good but wonder how you would ever find time for them. After all, some days are so busy you barely have time to eat or sleep. You also need time to relax.

How is it possible to juggle all of our needs and responsibilities and still continue to grow spiritually? I believe it comes down to

51

setting priorities. We basically find time for what is important to us. I encourage you to draw close to your Heavenly Father and to make time for Him. He wants to walk on this journey with you, giving you strength and courage for each day. May God bless you as you seek to nurture your relationship with Him!

When we take time to nourish our soul by meditating on God's Word and seeking Him in prayer, we can soar above the difficulties in life. Our hearts are nurtured, and we flourish in His presence!

How blessed is the man who does not walk in the counsel of the wicked, Nor stand in the path of sinners, Nor sit in the seat of scoffers! But his delight is in the law of the Lord, And in His law he meditates day and night. He will be like a tree *firmly* planted by streams of water, Which yields its fruit in its season and its leaf does not wither; And in whatever he does, he prospers.

Psalm 1:1–3 (NASB)

I have not departed from the command of His lips; I have treasured the words of His mouth more than my necessary food.

Job 23:12 (NASB)

Seek the Lord and His strength; Seek His face continually.

1 Chronicles 16:11 (NASB)

Reflections

1. Identify areas in your spiritual growth that have been put on the back burner while juggling the needs of your child.

   _____

   _____

   _____

   _____

2. How does feeding your soul strengthen you as you walk this journey with your child?

   _____

   _____

   _____

   _____

3. What are some ways you can continue to make your relationship with God a priority in your life?

   _____

   _____

   _____

   _____

Chapter 14

Enjoying Your Child

A happy heart makes the face cheerful,

—Proverbs 15:13a (NIV)

Maybe you are coming to the end of a school year and are feeling some anxiety. You may be asking, "What am I going to do with my child all summer?" My answer is, "Enjoy your child!" You also may be wondering how you will be able to provide enough structure for him or her.

Although children with autism seem to do much better with structure, they also thrive on physical activity and relaxation. Summer offers the opportunity for more physical activity and relaxation within the structure of home and family life. Although many parents work and require summer childcare or special programs, many of you will be at home with your child.

I hope you will look forward to this time to enjoy your child. It does take some thought and planning for you and your child to have an enjoyable summer. You may want to find community activities that are geared to his needs—possibly swimming lessons or a summer camp. Be sure to plan special outings that you can go on together, such as the zoo or a park. It can be as simple as a family picnic or a bike ride. Just use your imagination.

Remember to laugh together. It will do your heart good and heal your soul. Utilize this time to shower attention on your child, helping him feel loved and important.

Since children with autism like routine, I have a few simple ones that cause my grandson to break out in laughter every time. He has found a few for me as well. I often sing "You Are My Sunshine" when I first pick him up for a visit. I stop and let him fill in certain phrases. For example, "You are my _____." He has played along with this for years, and it has been a way for me to interact and connect with him. Now that he's a bit older, he may say, "No," when I start singing. When I continue, he breaks out in laughter and then sings along. Because he has outgrown this a bit, it has now become a joke between us.

We also drive along listening to *The Jungle Book* CD. During the song where Baloo is scratching his back on a tree, my grandson and I ring out, "Scratchy," and wiggle around as though we're scratching our backs on our car seats. I'm not sure what people driving by think of us, but we laugh and have fun!

My prayer is that God will bless your summer as you enjoy the precious gift of time with your child. Laugh and have fun!

I will always remember the wise words of my grandfather when I was expecting my first child, "You are going to find that your children will bring you the greatest enjoyment in life." Having raised four of his own, I trusted that he knew what he was talking about. And he was right!

He settles the childless woman in her home as a happy mother of children. Praise the Lord.

Psalm 113:9 (NIV)

A woman giving birth to a child has pain because her time has come; but when her baby is born she forgets the anguish because of her joy that a child is born into the world.

John 16:21 (NIV)

Grandchildren are the crown of old men, And the glory of sons is their father.

Proverbs 17:6 (NASB)

Reflections

1. What are some things you enjoy about your child?

   _____

   _____

   _____

   _____

2. What are some available activities in your community that are geared to your child's special needs?

   _____

   _____

   _____

   _____

3. Write about some situations where you and your child are able to laugh together on a regular basis.

   _____

   _____

   _____

   _____

Chapter 15

Communicating with Your Child

Call to me and I will answer you...

—Jeremiah 33:3a (NIV)

I often hear parents of children with autism say, "I wish we could communicate with each other." You just might be surprised at how well you and your child may be able to communicate! First of all, you have to get away from any preconceived perceptions of how it *should be.* When you do this, you free yourself and your child from unrealistic expectations that set both of you up for failure.

I honestly feel that I constantly communicate with my little grandson when he is with me. I've always carefully observed him and can usually anticipate his needs. With that being said, I still have to allow him to ask for what he wants.

My grandson and I communicate with hugs, kisses, and little expressions that I start and he finishes. For example, I say, "I love you." He says, "To the moon." If he's been quiet for a while, I may draw him out by singing one of his favorite songs and pausing to give him a chance to chime in. We also use his favorite hand puppets to play and communicate. Now that he's older, he is able to use complete sentences, answer questions and respond to requests at his *own* developmental level. What I'm trying to say is—know your child and always find creative ways to communicate with him or her.

Many children with autism are content to entertain themselves or to delve into their iPads. Don't make the mistake of thinking they don't want to communicate with you. They may even move to another room when you try to insert yourself into their activities. The key is to be present, wait for a pause, and then join them by showing interest in what they are doing.

I practiced this with my grandson during his weekly sleepover at my house. That particular morning, he was playing an iPad game, and I was working on a blog post on my iPhone. It became obvious that he wanted my attention because he put the iPad right in front of my face a few times to show me what he was doing. I know I could have corrected him, but I took this as his way of communicating with me. And I will always welcome his initiation of interaction.

I am aware that some children with autism are nonverbal and require more involved assistance to communicate. But as you become more familiar with your child, you will find nonverbal ways to communicate while he works toward becoming more verbal. Speech therapists can be of assistance in this area. Art therapy has also been effective in helping children express themselves through drawing or painting. I have also observed that many children with autism are drawn to music and may benefit from music therapy.

May God give you courage and strength as you learn to communicate with your very special child. May your interactions be as enjoyable and delightful as I have found them to be with my very special grandchild.

The manner in which we communicate with our children affects how they will respond to us. Our gracious, loving interaction will encourage them to open up rather than to withdraw.

> Everyone should be quick to listen, slow to speak and slow to become angry,
>
> James 1:19b (NIV)

> A word fitly spoken *is like* apples of gold in pictures of silver.
>
> Proverbs 25:11 (KJV)

> Let your speech always be with grace, *as though* seasoned with salt, so that you will know how you should respond to each person.
>
> Colossians 4:6 (NASB)

Reflections

1. How do you feel about the manner in which you communicate with your child?

   _____

   _____

   _____

   _____

2. Can you identify any unrealistic expectations you may have when trying to communicate?

   _____

   _____

   _____

   _____

3. In what ways do you *join* your child in order to draw him out?

   _____

   _____

   _____

   _____

Chapter 16

Finding Your Child's Spark

We have different gifts, according to the grace given to each of us.

—Romans 12:6a (NIV)

Yes, find his spark! We all have one, or two, or three and so does your child. The more he is given the opportunity to develop his interests, the more he will improve in other areas. It is a mistake to become so involved in the seriousness of autism that you fail to let your child just be a kid.

You will find that most children with autism are more similar to neurotypical children than they are different. They want to play and have fun. They like to swim, jump on a trampoline, and play in the park. Some love trains and cars while others like to sing and play instruments. Your child may excel in a certain sport or be an avid reader of books about a particular subject.

Whatever his spark may be, go for it! I mean, *really* go for it! Show genuine interest in what piques his interest. Praise him! Encourage and invest your time to help him pursue a hobby, sport, or talent. If you are able to spend a little money, do it if that is what is needed to expand his horizons.

If you haven't figured out what your child finds exciting or excels in, provide him with opportunities to explore different things. Use your imagination and observe him as he tries new activities. Really get to know your child and allow him to thrive and to find enjoyment in life. This can make all the difference in the world for a child with autism. He will develop a new sense of himself and become more confident. It can boost his mood and even help with socialization. Remember, he is, first and foremost, a child—a child who needs parents to help him *find his spark*!

We all have unique God-given interests, talents, and gifts. Part of the great adventure in life is discovering those gifts in ourselves and in our children. It can be a delightful experience!

As each one has received a *special* gift, employ it in serving one another as good stewards of the manifold grace of God.

1 Peter 4:10 (NASB)

To these four young men God gave knowledge and understanding of all kinds of literature and learning.

Daniel 1:17a (NIV)

Then Moses said to the sons of Israel, "See, the Lord has called by name Bezalel the son of Uri, the son of Hur, of the tribe of Judah. And he has filled him with the Spirit of God, in wisdom, in understanding, and in knowledge and in all kinds of craftsmanship; to make designs for working in gold and in silver and in bronze, and in the cutting of stones for settings and in the carving of wood, so as to perform in every inventive work."

Exodus 35:30–33 (NASB)

Reflections

1. In what ways have you shown enthusiasm about your child's unique interests?

_____

_____

_____

_____

2. What can you do to help your child discover his spark?

_____

_____

_____

_____

3. What is your child's spark?

_____

_____

_____

_____

Chapter 17

Helping Your Child Socialize

Practice hospitality.

—Romans 12:13b (NIV)

Socialization skills are probably difficult for your child. In fact, that is one of the diagnostic criteria for autism. Since neurotypical children need a little help from their parents in this, it only makes sense that a child with autism needs it even more. Yet many parents are so bogged down with treatments and schedules, they forget to help their children make friends.

You may be asking, "How can I help my child with this?" It can be as simple as setting up a playdate with another child. Getting to know the parents of your child's classmates is helpful. Become involved in community activities for children with special needs. It takes some extra effort to reach out to other families but the rewards are well worth it.

You can also encourage socialization with the parents of neurotypical children who know your child. My grandson has greatly benefited from playdates with the grandchild of a wonderful woman who volunteered in his home therapy program. She knew and understood my grandson enough to help her own grandchild understand him as well. They have had many fun times together swimming and playing in bounce houses at each other's birthday parties. Each boy has benefited by feeling loved and enjoyed by both families.

I encourage you to make the extra effort that is necessary to help your child make friends. You'll be glad you did!

Friendships add so much pleasure and satisfaction to our lives. A good friend is truly one of life's richest blessings. May you and your child experience the joy of spending time with friends.

A friend loves at all times,

Proverbs 17:17a (NASB)

Perfume and incense bring joy to the heart, and the pleasantness of a friend springs from their heartfelt advice.

Proverbs 27:9 (NIV)

Do not forsake your friend or a friend of your family,

Proverbs 27:10a (NIV)

Reflections

1. What are some specific ways you can help your child make friends?

   _____

   _____

   _____

   _____

2. What obstacles have you faced while helping your child socialize with other children?

   _____

   _____

   _____

   _____

3. What are some of the rewards you and your child have experienced as a result of building enjoyable relationships with others?

   _____

   _____

   _____

   _____

Chapter 18

Siblings and Cousins

Be devoted to one another in brotherly love; give preference
to one another in honor;

—Romans 12:10 (NASB)

Over the years, I have counseled siblings of children with autism.
They have their own set of blessings and challenges as they grow
up alongside their special needs brother or sister. Most of them
report a deep love and a sense of protectiveness toward their
sibling. They also talk about the challenges they face as the bulk
of their family's time and attention naturally gravitates toward the
child who appears to need it the most.

Unfortunately, neurotypical siblings may, on occasion, feel as
though they are growing up in the background while their sibling
with autism takes center stage. Although siblings are a great
support system, they may come to resent the extra responsibility
they often carry within the family. As you can see, it is a mixed
bag. Siblings may have mixed feelings and sometimes carry a sense
of guilt over their conflicting emotions. Individual and family
therapy can be beneficial to help them understand that these
feelings are normal for their situation.

There are often similar dynamics with cousins of a child with autism, but since they are not living in the same household, these dynamics are usually less intense. They are loving and protective but may also feel annoyed by certain mannerisms or behaviors of a cousin who has autism. Again, conflicted feelings.

It is my prayer that siblings and cousins of children with autism will receive the understanding and guidance they need to find their special place in the family. May God give you wisdom as you courageously work together to strengthen your family relationships.

Brotherly love among siblings and cousins is a beautiful thing. Your child is truly blessed to have these supportive relationships.

Behold, how good and how pleasant it is For brothers to dwell together in unity!

Psalm 133:1 (NASB)

Treat others the same way you want them to treat you.

Luke 6:31 (NASB)

To sum up, all of you be harmonious, sympathetic, brotherly, kindhearted, and humble in spirit;

1 Peter 3:8 (NASB)

Reflections

1. How have your child's siblings or cousins adjusted to their role in the family?

_____
_____
_____
_____

2. In what ways do you see their lives being blessed?

_____
_____
_____
_____

3. What are their greatest challenges?

_____
_____
_____
_____

Chapter 19

Advocating for Your Child

Don't let anyone look down on you because you are young,
—1 Timothy 4:12a (NIV)

You are your child's advocate. There is no getting around it, regardless of your age, education, or experience. You will fulfill this role over and over for your child throughout his or her life, beginning with the early intervention team.

Many young parents feel overwhelmed with school IEP (Individual Education Plan) meetings and psychological test results. They may be reluctant to speak up and give their opinion. If this is you, I want to encourage you, by all means, to speak up! You know your child better than anyone else. You are his best advocate.

There will be times when you disagree with a teacher's approach or attitude toward your child or a therapist's recommendations. When this happens, firmly and respectfully advocate for him. Others will listen to your concerns more openly and not become defensive if you approach them in a calm and reasonable manner.

If others perceive you as overly emotional or irrational, you will not be as effective.

May God give you the strength and courage you need to fulfill this important role in your child's life. May He give you wisdom as you advocate for your child!

Your children need you to speak for them, to protect them, and to look out for their best interests. May you continue to seek God's direction as you fulfill this important role.

Plans fail for lack of counsel, but with many advisers they succeed.

Proverbs 15:22 (NIV)

Open your mouth for the mute, For the rights of all the unfortunate. Open your mouth, judge righteously, And defend the rights of the afflicted and needy.

Proverbs 31:8–9 (NASB)

"See that you do not despise one of these little ones, for I say to you that their angels in heaven continually see the face of My Father who is in heaven."

Matthew 18:10 (NASB)

Reflections

1. How can you be your child's advocate?

_____

_____

_____

_____

2. What obstacles have you encountered as your child's advocate in the school setting?

_____

_____

_____

_____

3. How would you describe your level of confidence when speaking for your child and looking out for his best interests?

_____

_____

_____

_____

Chapter 20

What about Discipline?

Fathers, do not exasperate your children; instead, bring them up in the training and instruction of the Lord.

—Ephesians 6:4 (NIV)

As a grandmother of a child with autism, I'm not always the best resource on discipline. I have to admit that I'd rather enjoy and spoil my grandson a bit. Typical grandmother!

But I am aware that some form of structure and discipline is necessary for my grandson's well-being. So I have been known to give redirection as needed and even an occasional time-out. Although a child's parents are his main disciplinarians, grandparents have to follow through on their watch as well.

Some children with autism appear to be misbehaving or having a meltdown when they are, in reality, experiencing sensory overload. As a parent, you need to be aware of this in order to handle the situation appropriately. Give your child a sensory break to calm down rather than oppose him. Children can become oppositional if their parents are harsh and controlling in these types of situations. At times, you have to allow your child to say, "No," to get a clear picture of what he or she needs at that moment. I usually ask for a, "No, please."

But there are other times when traditional discipline is called for—when your child simply wants to get out of schoolwork or is acting inappropriately because he isn't getting his way. Of course discipline is needed when there is a safety issue such as running out into the street when you have told him to stop. Just remember that you are trying to lovingly discipline your child and not exasperate him. If discipline is handled appropriately, you will find your child with autism to be quite compliant most of the time.

I know the responsibility of disciplining your child may feel overwhelming at times. I hope you will seek God's wisdom as you lovingly provide the structure and discipline your child needs.

It is not a question of whether or not you should discipline your child, but that you lovingly discipline in a way that is appropriate to his special needs. Your child with autism needs your direction in his life. He has much to learn from you!

Discipline your children, and they will give you peace; they will bring you the delights you desire.

Proverbs 29:17 (NIV)

Listen, my son, to your father's instruction and do not forsake your mother's teaching. They are a garland to grace your head and a chain to adorn your neck.

Proverbs 1:8–9 (NIV)

… because the Lord disciplines those he loves, as a father the son he delights in.

Proverbs 3:12 (NIV)

Reflections

1. In what ways do you and your mate agree on how to discipline your child? In what ways do you disagree?

_____

_____

_____

_____

2. What are some preventative measures you have used to avoid behavioral issues or sensory meltdowns with your child?

_____

_____

_____

_____

3. How important do you feel it is to provide your child with appropriate and consistent structure?

_____

_____

_____

_____

Chapter 21

Eye Contact

I will instruct thee and teach thee in the way which thou shalt
go: I will guide thee with mine eye.

—Psalm 32:8 (KJV)

Eye contact is a special thing when you have a child with
autism. Early on, it will become obvious that your child will not
comfortably make eye contact with you. For a parent, this can be
difficult because you long to connect and look lovingly into his
eyes. Don't let this discourage you. Over time, he will most likely
become more comfortable looking at you for more than a fleeting
moment. Each time will feel like a special gift.

There are definitely some things you can do to facilitate
increased eye contact with your child. First of all, make sure you
always make eye contact when you are speaking to him, even if
he is not reciprocating at the moment. And be sure to smile as
often as you can.

You can also play interactive games that get his attention and
motivate him to look at you. I have been known to wear a silly
hat or my favorite—the purple octopus head piece—to spark my

grandson's interest. I let him have a turn at wearing his favorite one as well.

May God bless your efforts as you patiently continue to look for ways to connect with your child. It is such a joy to see a child respond to our gentle attempts to enter his or her world, in order to bring that child back into ours. I am certain you both will find the process delightful.

Our eyes are very important to us and play a vital role in communication. Helping your child with eye contact will enhance his ability to focus and connect with you and with the outside world.

"The eye is the lamp of the body;"

Matthew 6:22a (NASB)

The hearing ear and the seeing eye, The Lord has made both of them.

Proverbs 20:12 (NASB)

Behold, as the eyes of servants *look* to the hand of their master, As the eyes of a maid to the hand of her mistress, So our eyes *look* to the Lord our God, Until He is gracious to us.

Psalm 123:2 (NASB)

Reflections

1. What improvements would you like to see in your child's eye contact?

_____

_____

_____

_____

2. What specific things have helped your child improve his eye contact with you?

_____

_____

_____

_____

3. How consistent are you at making eye contact with your child when you are communicating with him?

_____

_____

_____

_____

Chapter 22

Special Diet and Supplements

Give us this day our daily bread.

—Matthew 6:11 (NASB)

Many children on the spectrum seem to benefit from special diets and supplements. Some have found a gluten-free and casein-free diet to be beneficial. Gluten is found in wheat, barley, and rye. Casein protein is found in dairy products.

If you are seeking specific dietary recommendations, it is helpful to consult with a medical doctor who specializes in autism and utilizes a biomedical approach. I have seen very positive results when a child is properly tested and prescribed an individualized protocol, including specific supplements.

Following these recommendations can be challenging for any family, but you can do it! Most supermarkets carry gluten-free items, and health food stores offer a wide variety of choices. Many restaurants now offer gluten-free choices as well. You will still feel somewhat limited at times. My grandson also has a peanut allergy, so we stick to a few cafes that are safe for him.

If your child stays with grandparents overnight, it is important to educate them on what he can eat. Sometimes it is helpful to send the special items along. Most grandparents, including me, like to please their child and give him treats. This is usually harmless for a typical child but can throw things off-balance for a child with autism. I have learned to keep small boxes of raisins on hand as a healthy snack instead of cookies or candy.

As a parent, it will require a little extra thought, planning, and organization to provide your child's *daily bread*. May God bless your efforts as you lovingly and courageously care for your child.

Stephanie Murphy

Proverbs 31 gives us an example of a virtuous woman. Among her many qualities, providing food to her household is mentioned along with bringing her food from afar. At times, you may feel that you are literally bringing your child's food *from afar*, as you seek to provide him with the nutrients needed to function at his best. May God bless you as you go the extra mile on a daily basis for your child with autism.

She is like merchant ships; She brings her food from afar.

Proverbs 31:14 (NASB)

She rises also while it is still night And gives food to her household…

Proverbs 31:15a (NASB)

She looks well to the ways of her household, And does not eat the bread of idleness.

Proverbs 31:27 (NASB)

Reflections

1. In what ways do you make your child's special dietary and supplemental needs a priority?

   _____

   _____

   _____

   _____

2. What obstacles have you successfully overcome to ensure that your child's special dietary needs are met?

   _____

   _____

   _____

   _____

3. How have you educated grandparents and extended family members about the importance of cooperating with your child's dietary protocol?

   _____

   _____

   _____

   _____

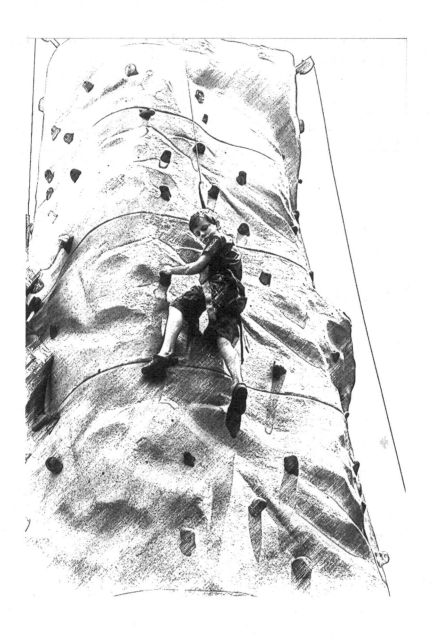

Chapter 23

Developmental Delays

There is a time for everything, and a season for every activity under the heavens:

—Ecclesiastes 3:1 (NIV)

At some point you may find yourself asking in exasperation, "Will I be changing diapers forever?" Although many children with autism are somewhat delayed when it comes to potty training, it won't be forever! I remember wondering if we would ever achieve success in our efforts with my own grandson.

I want to encourage you to be patient with your child during this time. It is important not to damage his self-esteem. Always remember that your child feels more than he is able to express. You don't want to set up an oppositional behavior pattern by getting into a power struggle with him.

Although there are many children's books and videos available to assist with potty training, they may not work with your child. If you are having a particularly difficult time, you may want to consider seeking the assistance of a therapist. One visit helped my grandson's family get on the same page and consistently use the positive reinforcement of watching something he loved on his iPad. For him, it was Japanese high-speed trains. Just find something that is a strong, positive reinforcement for your child and be sure each family member, including each grandparent, follows the same protocol. You may be surprised at just how quickly your efforts bring success.

There will be other areas where your child does not meet the developmental markers at the same time as his peers—and that's okay! Keep working with him and never give up on him! He will be riding his bicycle before you know it. Look out, because he'll take off one day and surprise you with his courage and ability!

May God bless you and your family as you joyfully embrace each season and time of growth in your lives.

May God bless your child with strength as he reaches each developmental milestone and accomplishment. May you rejoice with him as his confidence increases and his spirit soars!

> I can do all things through Him who strengthens me.
>
> Philippians 4:13 (NASB)

> But he said to me, "My grace is sufficient for you, for my power is made perfect in weakness."
>
> 2 Corinthians 12:9 (NIV)

> The Sovereign Lord is my strength; he makes my feet like the feet of deer, he enables me to tread on the heights.
>
> Habakkuk 3:19 (NIV)

Reflections

1. What feelings have you struggled with regarding any developmental delays your child may have?

_____

_____

_____

_____

2. In what ways have you been successful in communicating acceptance, patience, and encouragement to your child as he reaches developmental milestones at his own pace?

_____

_____

_____

_____

3. What attitudes and beliefs can you cultivate to help joyfully embrace each season of growth in your child's life?

_____

_____

_____

_____

Chapter 24

Read, Read, Read!

The heart of the discerning acquires knowledge, for the ears
of the wise seek it out.

—Proverbs 18:15 (NIV)

I can't stress enough how important it is going to be for you to read
books about autism. Some have been authored by families, like
yours, who are walking this journey and wanting to share their
experiences. Others are written by medical doctors, including
those who have children of their own on the spectrum. They
have researched and used their medical expertise to give direction.
There are books about specific treatments and programs that have
been successful for some children.

You don't want to set out on this path alone or in the dark.
Even if you aren't an avid reader, I want to encourage you to
become one. When my grandson was first diagnosed with autism,
I began to read every book about the subject that I could get my
hands on. I would have a stack of five or six at a time on my
nightstand.

Most of us have a very limited knowledge of autism until
our own families are touched by it. Even professionals, although

trained in the clinical aspects, have no way of grasping all of the emotional nuances or family dynamics that are involved without personally experiencing them. This experience is too important to rely solely on the advice of others. It is *your* loved one, and you will want to become as knowledgeable as you can in order to make the best decisions possible for your child.

May God bless you as you seek knowledge about autism through reading. You and your child will both benefit as you integrate this wisdom into your lives.

The book of Proverbs emphasizes the importance of obtaining wisdom and understanding. You will benefit from reading about the experiences of others and from acquainting yourself with the current research on autism. May God give you wisdom as you endeavor to sort through and utilize this knowledge.

> Do not forsake wisdom, and she will protect you; love her, and she will watch over you.
>
> Proverbs 4:6 (NIV)

> Hold on to instruction, do not let it go; guard it well, for it is your life.
>
> Proverbs 4:13 (NIV)

> A wise man will hear and increase in learning, And a man of understanding will acquire wise counsel.
>
> Proverbs 1:5 (NASB)

Reflections

1. What books have been the most helpful to you as you have tried to understand the complexities of autism?

_____

_____

_____

_____

2. What specific information has been the most beneficial?

_____

_____

_____

_____

3. How difficult has it been for your spouse or other family members to understand the importance of doing their own reading and research?

_____

_____

_____

_____

Chapter 25

Adapting to Your Child

> ... do not *merely* look out for your own personal interests, but also for the interests of others.
>
> —Philippians 2:4 (NASB)

As a parent, you will be looking out for the interests of your child. But raising a child with autism requires you to adapt to his or her needs on a daily basis. Life gets easier once you accept this. Acceptance does away with the tendency we all have to complain about something that causes us a little more effort or work.

Many children with autism have difficulty with loud noises and cover their ears for protection. One young mother told me she asks her daughter to go into her bedroom while she vacuums. Then she races to complete the task as quickly as possible in order to minimize her child's discomfort. She's adapting!

As you accept your child and his special needs, you will find yourself naturally and lovingly adapting on a daily basis. It can be something as simple as letting him know you are about to use the blender and giving him the choice of removing himself from the noise. There may be times when you have to exit a particularly noisy restaurant if you notice your child is experiencing sensory overload.

Being adaptable doesn't mean you never give your child the opportunity to adjust. In fact, taking him places and exposing him to different settings can also help, as long as you are willing to leave the situation if he becomes overwhelmed. This gradual exposure, coupled with his sense of security in your love and care, will result in having a child who can go almost anywhere. May God bless your efforts as you endeavor to adapt to your child.

Your child will thrive in an atmosphere of respect and acceptance as you make the effort to adapt to his special needs. You will be blessed as you choose to have an attitude of contentment and cheerfulness.

> Not that I speak from want, for I have learned to be content in whatever circumstances I am.
>
> Philippians 4:11 (NASB)

> Show proper respect to everyone,
>
> 1 Peter 2:17a (NIV)

> Accept one another, then, just as Christ accepted you, in order to bring praise to God.
>
> Romans 15:7 (NIV)

Reflections

1. In what specific ways have you adapted to your child's special needs?

   _____

   _____

   _____

   _____

2. What attitudes have been helpful as you have tried to adapt to your child in positive and accepting ways?

   _____

   _____

   _____

   _____

3. Are there times when you give your child the opportunity to adapt and adjust to specific situations?

   _____

   _____

   _____

   _____

Chapter 26

Choosing Not to Be Overwhelmed

> From the end of the earth will I cry unto thee, when my heart is overwhelmed: lead me to the rock that is higher than I.
>
> —Psalm 61:2 (KJV)

The sooner you make the choice not to be overwhelmed, the happier you will be! As a parent of a special needs child, you will have plenty of opportunities to feel overwhelmed by your circumstances. You may find yourself being hypervigilant on an almost moment by moment basis as you try to keep your child safe and secure. So you ask, "What do I do to not feel overwhelmed?"

It seems to boil down to a choice—choosing peace over worry and faith over doubt. Scripture tells us that God will keep us in perfect peace if we keep our mind stayed on Him. As a clinical therapist for many years, I helped my patients learn to take control of their negative thinking patterns so they could feel more positive. They achieved a greater sense of well-being and peace. However, human insight has never promised the *perfect peace* that God says He will give us.

You can be sure God cares about you. He sees your hurts and your difficulties but is with you. If you will look to Him for courage and strength, you will find His peace. Take time for Him even in the midst of your busy schedule and endless responsibilities. He will meet you where you are and give you peace!

When you are feeling overwhelmed by your circumstances, I encourage you to move your focus from the problem to God's love and peace. Remember just how big God is. We find His peace when we walk in the present with our big God—with our God who can do anything!

Finally, brethren, whatever is true, whatever is honorable, whatever is right, whatever is pure, whatever is lovely, whatever is of good repute, if there is any excellence and if anything worthy of praise, dwell on these things.

Philippians 4:8 (NASB)

...casting all your anxiety on Him, because He cares for you.

1 Peter 5:7 (NASB)

Finally, my brethren, be strong in the Lord, and in the power of his might.

Ephesians 6:10 (KJV)

Reflections

1. How difficult is it for you to choose not to be overwhelmed?

_____

_____

_____

_____

2. In what situations are you looking to God for strength and peace?

_____

_____

_____

_____

3. What are some ways you can take control of your thought patterns in order to feel more positive?

_____

_____

_____

_____

Chapter 27

Be Thankful

Rejoice always; pray without ceasing; in everything give
thanks; for this is God's will for you in Christ Jesus.

—1 Thessalonians 5:16–18 (NASB)

First of all, I want to say that I know it is not always easy to have
a thankful heart. When life becomes stressful, it is easy to give in
to feelings of hopelessness. Yet it is in our thankfulness that we
find renewed strength and hope.

I recently spoke with a Christian man who shared with me
that, at times, he and his wife struggled with angry feelings
toward God. He said, "Why did God choose someone like me
who doesn't earn enough money to pay for all of my son's needs?
I work all the hours I can possibly work and it still isn't enough.
Government scholarships are only a drop in the bucket." My
heart went out to him as I thought about how my own daughter
and son-in-law have taken on extra work to pay for expensive
therapies.

All parents want the best for their children. They want to
be able to provide adequately for their needs. Yet the needs of
children with autism far outweigh most parents' income. These

parents can either become discouraged and bitter or they can choose to be thankful in the midst of their difficulties. It becomes a choice, and this choice will affect their happiness and quality of life.

Again, I know it is difficult. It takes faith in God's providence and trust in His love and care for us. We can't always accomplish this in our own power, so I want to encourage you to seek God's strength as you courageously choose to live a thankful life.

Scripture encourages us to give thanks in *every* situation. Faith and hope are renewed as we choose to be thankful, even in the midst of difficulty.

Giving thanks always for all things unto God and the Father in the name of our Lord Jesus Christ;

Ephesians 5:20 (KJV)

In everything give thanks: for this is the will of God in Christ Jesus concerning you.

1 Thessalonians 5:18 (KJV)

Do not be anxious about anything, but in every situation, by prayer and petition, with thanksgiving, present your requests to God.

Philippians 4:6 (NIV)

Reflections

1. How has the everyday stress of parenting a child with autism affected your feelings of thankfulness?

   _____

   _____

   _____

   _____

2. What are you most thankful for?

   _____

   _____

   _____

   _____

3. In what ways do you trust in God's providence, love, and care for you?

   _____

   _____

   _____

   _____

Chapter 28

Be Your Child's Spiritual Leader

Train up a child in the way he should go, even when he is old he will not depart from it.

—Proverbs 22:6 (NASB)

My nine-year-old grandson attended his church's Vacation Bible School this summer. A tall, smiling, teenage boy was by his side each afternoon when I arrived to pick him up. He was his *buddy*. This young man had been trained and assigned to our special needs child to give him the opportunity to participate in Vacation Bible School, right alongside all of the other children.

Later in the day when I asked my grandson which movie he would like to see, he immediately responded, "The Jesus Movie." So we watched his children's movie about the life of Christ. He had already watched it numerous times over the past few years, but today, he seemed to have a new interest in it.

Later that week, I noticed him intently watching and listening to Bible stories on his iPad as we rode along in the car. It was only last week that he had been routinely playing the *Angry Birds* game instead. Was this new interest in Bible stories a result of his recent experiences at Vacation Bible School? I believe so! You see,

I know him well. I know his patterns and routines, and this was definitely different.

My point is, please don't underestimate your child's capacity to learn about Jesus. Your child understands far more than he or she is able to communicate. We are aware of this in other areas of my grandson's life. He absorbs information like a sponge, often memorizes it, and never forgets it. Why wouldn't this be true for spiritual things as well? In fact, my grandson has memorized several Bible verses over the years and never seems to forget them.

Throughout your child's life, many people will influence him in one way or another, but you, as the parent, will have the greatest influence. Why not influence him spiritually by lovingly teaching your child about his Creator and Savior. Don't assume that it is too much for him to grasp. Why not take his hand and gently lead him to Christ?

May God bless you as you seek to be your child's spiritual leader and guide.

You are your child's spiritual leader. May God bless you as you give your child the opportunity to know Jesus and to learn about the Bible.

These commandments that I give you today are to be on your hearts. Impress them on your children. Talk about them when you sit at home and when you walk along the road, when you lie down and when you get up.

Deuteronomy 6:6–7 (NIV)

I have hidden your word in my heart that I might not sin against you.

Psalm 119:11 (NIV)

… and that from childhood you have known the sacred writings which are able to give you the wisdom that leads to salvation through faith which is in Christ Jesus.

2 Timothy 3:15 (NASB)

Reflections

1. How do you view your role as your child's spiritual leader?

_____

_____

_____

_____

2. In what ways has your child shown an interest in God, Bible stories, or creation?

_____

_____

_____

_____

3. What are some specific ways you can give your child the opportunity to know Jesus and to learn about the Bible?

_____

_____

_____

_____

Chapter 29

What If My Child Has Severe Autism?

Ah Lord God! Behold, You have made the heavens and the earth by Your great power and by Your outstretched arm! Nothing is too difficult for You,

—Jeremiah 32:17 (NASB)

"What if my child has severe autism?" is a hard question. You may think some of the topics I've talked about in this book don't apply to you. You may feel completely overwhelmed and hopeless. What I want you to know is that nothing is too hard for God! If you will invite Him to walk alongside you and your family on this journey, He promises to be with you.

Over the years, I have counseled several families who have had children with severe autism. Yes, it was difficult. Sometimes there were behavior problems and concerns about their children running away or being nonverbal. The safety issues were real and required constant supervision and watchfulness. Many parents experienced sadness when they felt they couldn't verbally communicate with their child.

If this is your situation, you are going to need the assistance of special programs and schools, respite workers, and other professionals. Think of them as valuable resources as you work together to give your child the best possible care. I have seen families who are able to function because of the support they have received from government, community, and family.

These resources won't necessarily come to you. It will require hours of research, phone calls, and filling out applications. Don't become discouraged! It will take time, and you may end up on a waiting list for some services. This requires perseverance and patience, but eventually, your hard work will pay off. Life will become more manageable as these services and benefits start to fall into place.

My prayer is that you will realize just how strong and courageous you are. May you lean on God, knowing that nothing is too difficult for Him.

It is reassuring to know that God is walking beside you as you and your family face the obstacles on your path. When you feel powerless over your circumstances, I encourage you to trust in His great power.

For with God nothing shall be impossible.

Luke 1:37 (KJV)

It is He who made the earth by His power, Who established the world by His wisdom; And by His understanding He has stretched out the heavens.

Jeremiah 10:12 (NASB)

"I know that you can do all things; no purpose of yours can be thwarted."

Job 42:2 (NIV)

Reflections

1. What feelings have been the most difficult for you to deal with as the parent of a child with severe autism?

_____

_____

_____

_____

2. What obstacles have required you to draw upon God's strength and your inner courage in a significant way?

_____

_____

_____

_____

3. What medical and community resources have been valuable in your search to provide the best possible care for your child?

_____

_____

_____

_____

Chapter 30

Long-Term Planning

A good man leaves an inheritance to his children's children,

—Proverbs 13:22a (NASB)

One mother, who had a child with severe autism, once told me she had learned to always hope for the best but to plan for the worst. Your first impression of this statement might be that she didn't have much faith for her child's future, but that wasn't the case at all. This mother had to be stronger and more courageous than she ever dreamed she could be.

Year after year, I watched as she consistently advocated for services for her child and tried numerous therapies to help him reach his full potential. I also saw her plan for his future in the event she or her husband might no longer be on this earth to care for him. This was wise and loving planning. It is what we need to do for our loved ones who have autism.

I encourage you to meet with your family attorney to discuss the legal aspects of providing for your child after you are gone. It is important to take these steps early on, regardless of your age. If you are a young parent, you may want to look at term life insurance coverage, since it is relatively inexpensive. Your attorney will be able to give you professional guidance on setting up a special needs trust. Grandparents can do this as well if they are interested.

Some parents avoid this type of planning because it is too painful for them to deal with the possibility that their child might need long-term assistance. But you are taking a risk with your child's future if you are not doing some type of long-range planning. So I encourage you, once again, to take a deep breath of courage and to face these issues head on. It will give you peace of mind to know that you have made provision for your child's future.

May God strengthen your heart as you lovingly work through the details of leaving an inheritance for your child.

It is so important to plan for your child's future. Leaving an inheritance for your special needs child requires extra planning and preparation. May God direct you as you seek professional guidance to ensure a successful future for your child.

Houses and wealth are inherited from parents,

Proverbs 19:14a (NIV)

"Suppose one of you wants to build a tower. Won't you first sit down and estimate the cost to see if you have enough money to complete it?"

Luke 14:28 (NIV)

May he give you the desire of your heart and make all your plans succeed.

Psalm 20:4 (NIV)

Reflections

1. What specific steps have you taken to secure your child's financial future?

_____

_____

_____

_____

2. Can you identify any feelings or attitudes that may have hindered you from beginning the process of long-term planning?

_____

_____

_____

_____

3. What benefits do you see in taking action *now* to plan for your child's future?

_____

_____

_____

_____

Chapter 31

Tonight I Prayed for You

The effectual prayer of a righteous man can accomplish much.
—James 5:16b (NASB)

Most of us have someone we love and care about who needs a touch from God—an answer to prayer. Many of us have family members who have autism and we love them, so we fervently intercede in prayer for them.

My sweet grandson was diagnosed with autism several years ago, so I pray for him, night after night and year after year. I've seen him make much progress and I'm praying he will reach his God-given potential. My heart hurts when he hurts, so I can't help but pray. One thing I've come to realize is that God loves my grandson even more than I do, so I can trust Him with his care.

I encourage you not to be discouraged if your prayers aren't answered immediately or in the way you would like them to be. Trust in God's sovereignty and thank Him for what He is doing in your life and in the life of your loved one. On this journey, we grieve, accept, love, and seek help. We also pray because, deep in our souls, we know that God hears our fervent prayers. We know He is with us and that He works all things together for our good.

I wrote the following poem one night after I lay down with my little grandson to sing him to sleep. In fact, I've been singing him to sleep since he was two weeks old. I'm not really a singer, but the lyrics of "Amazing Grace" seem to lull him right to sleep. This particular night I felt such compassion for him. I laid my hand on his forehead as he slept and prayed.

Tonight I Prayed for You

Tonight I prayed for you,
My hand upon your head,
Asking God to bless you
As you slept in your bed.

Tonight I prayed for you,
My heart so moved with love,
Asking God to protect you
With His angels up above.

Tonight I prayed for you,
My kiss upon your cheek,
Asking God to guide you
And that His face you'll seek.

Tonight your Nana prayed for you,
My grandson my delight,
Asking God to give you courage
And to help you win this fight.

Tonight I prayed for you,
My faith in God above,
Asking Him to heal the autism
With outstretched hands of love.

A friend of mine, who also has a grandson with autism, once told me that he has prayed for his grandson every night for the past ten years. I want to encourage you to pray for your children every day. Never stop seeking God's face on their behalf.

> Confess *your* faults one to another, and pray one for another, that ye may be healed. The effectual fervent prayer of a righteous man availeth much.
>
> James 5:16 (KJV)

> But when you pray, go into your room, close the door and pray to our Father, who is unseen. Then your Father who sees what is done in secret, will reward you.
>
> Matthew 6:6 (NIV)

> Then you will call upon Me and come and pray to Me, and I will listen to you. You will seek Me and find Me when you search for Me with all your heart.
>
> Jeremiah 29:12–13 (NASB)

Reflections

1. What feelings have you had regarding God's answers to your prayers for your child?

   _____

   _____

   _____

   _____

2. How difficult is it for you to trust God's sovereignty and timing as you pray for your child?

   _____

   _____

   _____

   _____

3. How secure are you in God's love for you and your family and in His promise that all things work together for our good?

   _____

   _____

   _____

   _____

Chapter 32

Arms of Love

Beloved, let us love one another, for love is from God; and
everyone who loves is born of God and knows God.

—1 John 4:7 (NASB)

As a church, we need to put our arms of love around families
touched by autism. They are often isolated and struggling under
challenges that outweigh their resources. Many do not have
extended family living nearby and have lost the social support of
friends who simply do not know how to deal with autism. They
need our emotional, social, and spiritual support—they need our
arms of love around them.

We can't assume their smiling faces mean everything is okay.
It's impossible to fully understand the impact of autism unless it
has touched your own family. But that is no excuse for apathy. We
can become more educated, compassionate, and involved. With
autism reaching epidemic proportions, we have a responsibility as
Christians to bring the needs of these families to light.

We don't have to wait for our churches to come up with special
programs. Most of us know at least one family who has been
touched by autism. We can take the initiative and get involved in

their lives, remembering that the time and energy demands they face are high. In other words, seek to lighten their load rather than having unrealistic expectations of what you should receive in return. They will be most grateful for your positive input in their lives.

I pray God's blessing on each of us as we seek to be an extension of His love to families touched by autism. May we open our hearts and reach out to them with arms of love!

As Christians, we are called to love others, to bear each other's burdens, and to share. This may take the form of giving our time, our resources, or our emotional support. Families touched by autism will benefit as we reach out to them in love.

Bear one another's burdens, and thereby fulfill the law of Christ.

Galatians 6:2 (NASB)

And do not neglect doing good and sharing, for with such sacrifices God is pleased.

Hebrews 13:16 (NASB)

He answered, "Love the Lord your God with all your heart and with all your soul and with all your strength and with all your mind; and, Love your neighbor as yourself."

Luke 10:27 (NIV)

Reflections

1. In what way has your church reached out to your family?

    _____

    _____

    _____

    _____

2. How can you help your church family become more educated about autism?

    _____

    _____

    _____

    _____

3. What is the most important way others can be an extension of God's love to you and your family?

    _____

    _____

    _____

    _____

Hope

As I see my grandson making strides in his development, I am hopeful for more to come. I remember a time when hope seemed dim in the early years after his diagnosis. During the early developmental stages, progress can be slow and inconsistent, but don't get discouraged. Never stop believing in your child and never, ever, give up hope.

Sometimes it's hard for parents to realize just how far their child has come because they are with him every day. It is helpful to put everything into perspective by reminding yourself of where he started and how far along he is today. Don't make the mistake of comparing him with other children. He's not competing with them. This is his journey!

So on those days when you're wondering if he will ever say more, become more social, or graduate from high school, take heart! He's not finished yet! Relax, accept him where he is today, and give him the love and encouragement he needs to reach his full potential!

Conclusion

My purpose for writing this book is to give hope and encouragement to families who have been touched by autism. Medical experts and educators may inadvertently take away our hope—our hope for healing and recovery, hope for our child's future, or hope for a reciprocal, loving parent-child relationship. I know they don't intentionally plan to dishearten us with their statistics and probabilities, nonetheless, it takes a toll on a parent's morale. It is no wonder many parents and family members struggle with depression after the dismal diagnosis of autism is handed to them. The professionals may explain that they don't want to give us false hope. They base it on the current view of autism in our society.

I hope this book has helped you tap into the healing power of God's love and into your love for your child. I have seen children with autism flourish, heal, and grow as a result of their family's loving interaction with them. Some of these children progress to very high levels of functioning, with only a few symptoms of autism remaining. Others progress more slowly. Regardless of the outcome, it is the journey that is important.

I believe every child is our teacher—especially our children with autism. I encourage you to open your heart and soul as you embark on this very unique and purposeful journey. Be prepared for change because nothing stays the same after your child is diagnosed with autism. Priorities drastically change! Family dynamics, your marital relationship, and relationships with friends all change. Finances and time commitments change as well.

Change is usually stressful, even if it's a positive one. So be prepared to manage each change in a thoughtful, rational, and calm manner. (I know that's easier said than done!) But also know that it's okay to cry, grieve, and feel totally stressed out at times. We are humans, and humans feel deeply. Don't be afraid of your feelings. Stuffing them only leads to an eruption somewhere down the road. It is important to have a good support system around you to laugh and cry with.

May God's love flow through you as you become an extension of His love to your child. May you grow through your experiences as you lovingly take the journey into your child's world in order to gently bring him out into yours. And never forget just how strong and courageous you are!

Be strong and courageous. Do not be afraid;
do not be discouraged, for the Lord your
God will be with you wherever you go.

Joshua 1:9 (NIV)

Invitation

"For God so loved the world, that He gave His only begotten Son, that whoever believes in Him shall not perish, but have eternal life."

—John 3:16 (NASB)

Sometimes people don't know what to say to God to begin a relationship with Him. Would you kindly consider using this prayer to help you? Just pray this in your mind and heart to God right now.

Dear God, I realize that I am a sinner, and I am very sorry for my sins. Please forgive me. I now believe that Jesus Christ is your Son, and that He gave His life as a sacrifice for me. Please come into my life and save me from my sins. Thank You for Your love for me. Amen.

Scriptures about Salvation

For by grace you have been saved through faith; and that not of yourselves, *it is* the gift of God; not as a result of works, so that no one may boast.

Ephesians 2:8–9 (NASB)

If you declare with your mouth, "Jesus is Lord," and believe in your heart that God raised him from the dead, you will be saved. For it is with your heart that you believe and are justified, and it is with your mouth that you profess your faith and are saved.

Romans 10:9–10 (NIV)

Therefore as you have received Christ Jesus the Lord, *so* walk in Him,

Colossians 2:6 (NASB)

"Go home to your own people and tell them how much the Lord has done for you, and how he has had mercy on you."

Mark 5:19b (NIV)

Appendix 1

Autism Resources

The resources on this page are not intended as a referral, endorsement, or recommendation but simply as references for you to do further research.

autismspeaks.org

autismnow.org

healautismnow.org

autism-society.org

autismtreatmentcenter.org

Appendix 2

Books about Autism

The book titles and authors listed on this page are not intended as a referral, endorsement, or recommendation but simply as references for you to do further research.

1. *Ten Things Every Child with Autism Wishes You Knew* by Ellen Notbohm

2. *Thinking in Pictures* by Temple Grandin

3. *The Spark* by Kristine Barnett

4. *Special Diets for Special Kids* by Lisa Lewis

5. *Son Rise: The Miracle Continues* by Barry Neil Kaufman

6. *Bright Not Broken, Gifted Kids, ADHD, and Autism* by Diane M. Kennedy & Rebecca S. Banks

7. *The Autistic Brain* by Temple Grandin and Richard Panek

8. *The Autism Acceptance Book, Being a Friend to Someone with Autism* by Ellen Sabin

9. *1001 Great Ideas for Teaching & Raising Children with Autism or Asperger's: Expanded 2nd Edition* by Ellen Notbohm and Veronica Zysk

10. *Understanding Samantha: A Sibling's Perspective of Autism* by Dustin Daniels

11. *Autism Solutions, How to Create a Healthy & Meaningful Life for Your Child* by Ricki G. Robinson, M.D., MPH

12. *Autism Life Skills* by Chantal Sicile-Kira

About the Author

Stephanie Murphy offers encouragement for families touched by autism. She draws, not only on her three decades of experience as a family therapist, but also on her personal experience as the grandmother of a child with autism. She has a master's degree in counseling and is a licensed marriage & family therapist. Stephanie also shares wisdom from God's word and from her own Christian faith. She is actively involved with her husband in his life's work as a missionary to young people in Europe. Having survived the death of a spouse she has learned to press into God during difficult circumstances and understands what it means to become *strong and courageous* in His strength.

Email Stephanie at: stephanieannmurphy@icloud.com

Visit her blog site at: stephanieannmurphy.com